The Melancholy of Anatomy

Also by Martin Corless-Smith

Poetry
The Fool & The Bee (Shearsman Books 2019)
Bitter Green (Fence Books 2015)
English Fragments: A Brief History of the Soul (Fence Books 2010)
Swallows (Fence Books 2006)
Nota (Fence Books 2003)
Complete Travels (West House Books 2000)
Of Piscator (University of Georgia Press 1998)

Prose / Essays
The Poet's Tomb (Parlor Press 2020)
The ongoing mystery of the disappearing self (SplitLevel Texts, 2020)
This Fatal Looking Glass (SplitLevel Texts 2015)

Translations
Odious Horizons: Some Versions of Horace (Miami University Press 2019)

Martin
Corless-Smith

*The Melancholy
of Anatomy*

Shearsman Books

First published in the United Kingdom in 2021 by
Shearsman Books Ltd
PO Box 4239
Swindon
SN3 9FN

Shearsman Books Ltd Registered Office
30–31 St. James Place, Mangotsfield, Bristol BS16 9JB
(this address not for correspondence)

www.shearsman.com

ISBN 978-1-84861-758-2

Copyright © Martin Corless-Smith, 2021.

The right of Martin Corless-Smith to be identified as the author
of this work has been asserted by him in accordance with the
Copyrights, Designs and Patents Act of 1988.
All rights reserved.

Contents

To the Muses	9
The Melancholy of Anatomy	
The Melancholy of Anatomy	17
The object observed (sn*w)	18
The Knight Adventurer	20
Salvator Mundi	21
Pareidolia	23
Coleridge's Window	24
Cycling in a cypress grove	25
poète maudit	26
Bible stories before bed	27
The Selve Obscured	29
The end of poetry	32
The ghost of Egremont appears	
in a snapshot of his favourite horse	33
Various late landscapes	34
(Sea Poems)	39
Letters from the Interior	51
Moments of Inertia	
Regarding the interior	61
Samson Beleaguered (His blindness/Death)	62
Coleridge's Mirror	64
Wreck of the Sisterland	65
The Turk's head	67
The Dardanelles	68
Unheimlich	69
Bathetic verse	70
Narcissus's scissors	71
'The heart is crazy in its cage'	72
The object observed (D**th)	73

The evening otherwise	74
The ghost of a poppy (Armistice Day, 2018)	75
'a gurgling barbarous…'	76
Song endings	77
Moments of inertia	89

The Bird Zone

Anonymous motorway café	97
The Rising (Lazarus)	101
The Falling (Daedalus)	102
(Misquoting the quotidian)	103
(Twilight summer)	104
The bird zone	105

for
T.C. Corless-Smith
(1930–2020)

I too feel the vast and shapeless melancholy of having been created. I'd rather have stayed in the immanescence of the sacred Nothing.

—Clarice Lispector, *A Breath of Life*

To the Muses

Hey qwerty I hear you
hoped to be important
turned out ordinary
thas ok. Wasn even kind
or do my best
those days when I lean out
and feel the passing truck
society is full of kids
who didn't ever get the balloon
see you on tv and hate myself

Oh qwerty can we count
ourselves into oblivion
she doesn't love me as I hoped
I can't seem to convince her
how the dogs are in a swoon
for god knows what reason
chewed the shoes and sausages
gave up myself a century ago
hilarious the vanity this jacket shows

When mother died
her open mouth had nothing fit to say
because there's nothing but the rattle
of the curtain beads to show our passage
from the nylon sheets
into the ether over recent
duck ponds where the invalids
are wheeled out for fresh air

Oh qwerty hear the cars
on Highway number whatever
and hear the geese ridiculous
on top of multi-storey buildings

honking incongruously
just like me is why the passing stranger
smiles because we both know we are dead
and no one loves us and the goose
has nothing quite as wrong as we do
stacking unassailable anxieties
with fervor borrowed from lost
histories abandoned half way through.

Oh qwerty under ice
The whalers cannot find the whales
nor can the eskimos
I'm tired against your face
we care about the future
out of superstition
that a moral tale might find us out

qwerty with your azure plastic cover
like the earth
from outerspace
the semi blackness of our sphere

I cried into a cup
How's that for performed sincerity
She wanted to break up with me
So thrilling I forgot to breathe.

Oh qwerty quiet on your bed
With pious disregard for my solicitations
how is a voice to wander
on this empty plane
unless you guide his wanton
hope. Scroll as we might
the future cannot raise an ear
until you call to her
faithless and immune
I like an accident

that gathers all these lines
am of no consequence
except for happening to register
a mere impression on the matter

qwerty in paris cairo rome
alone with the impossible
and infinite I'm bound
why I recall the names of schoolyard bullies
rather than the title of a favourite book
hold out your hand to strangers
just to feel rejection as a common bond
hail to the passing citi-cab
thrill in my anonymity
the Russians dream of mother Rus
the Danish with their haughty frowns
the Germans like a plate of wurst
the English fumble under eiderdowns.

qwerty curves in space and time
collapsing in synaptic voids
all alligators facing east
all litter coloured orange, red & green

what a mean is that we're alone
alive and thas impossible,
the subject organized
to make the most of this
which for some years has seemed
as if it were a trial I failed?
Are we afraid to no longer bee
To not hold out an arm to touch
The passing tree burns
as there's no
tomorrow
just a day (this one)
along the way to none

I sin a wasp
Size off my fingre
Sitting top a yellow fleur
It says to me tomorrow morning
I'm gone be dead
And you still here

One thousand *Götternamen*
crawling on the weedy stamen
totamque infusa per artus
mens agitat molem et magno se corpore miscet

There may be fire dancing on the screen
Dear qwerty fifty crews outmuscled by a spark
There is a drone that hovers over every noun
and when we smile we see ourselves on television
When I loved last century I had a bicycle to get me there
and now I'm sitting in the airport lounge,
trying not to see the daytime tv host ejaculate his praise
repeated every thirty minutes on a loop
until some other element is added to refresh the tape.

Hey qwerty it's impossible to say
to speak at all. I called the other day and heard myself
half a second afterwards, and knew it wasn't me.

Saw a sparrow didn't need
me drinking tea & eating lemon slice
Getting high and disappearing
Like old times and mother dear

Saying I never knew what
It felt like to be alive
The birds hop in the sapling &
I walk by and die *im Abendrot*

*

If you were raised as a girl
qwerty where is your body now?
if love was dropped from the basinet
onto the shining boards of the *salle à manger*

even an atom can find no home
its name around it like a satellite
who should a self pretend to find
craning in her cot, her toes entwined

*

cousin qwerty plays the Sybil cards
address the morning as you would a friend
a relative as such it is (of course)
she can't help but suffer true to type
and miserable we say and do in fragments
miserly withdrawn from common intercourse

If I had a table qwerty I would bend
you over it you nonexistent muse
and gingerly accuse you of my own desire
which muscled you out of the air

if I has a voice it is an echo
of your reckoning
and swallows spit to punctuate
the exhalations of my sobbing aria

*

reported missing Thursday night
we continue to follow
all leads and enquiries if the public
spectacle of loss and rhetoric that ends all hope

we ask the muse to help us answer
questions we have never asked
please don't hesitate in coming forward
a dedicated line has been set up

The Melancholy of Anatomy

The Melancholy of Anatomy

To analyse this motionary carcass thus:
I can't help noticing
the swayback dog's
caducous wandering

as my father regularly falls
conscious of his failed anatomy but
subject to a daily constitutional
wondering when he'll hit his limit or the floor.

The German word *"gefallen"*
indicates how beauty falls
upon the aesthete
irrespective of his will

feet might function
in our hero's quest
where moral strength ignores
the benefits of sensible retreat

(a fundamental paradox prevails
until resolved by its inevitable collapse).

The object observed (sn*w)

Whether to establish it as found
Or made—I crater to a fault
The intention to support a place
From which to look out from.
Flurried in the storm we might
Project our future home as recompense
But are we capable of making snow
In infinite variety as if to show
Uniqueness is the quality of now?
Conscious of the revelation
Of an-always-happening—such as
A snowstorm that reveals whilst covering
A pathless route part me part pathless route.

(Imagine a still lake reflecting snow
exactly at the instant that the snow
touched to its surface—there is no
need to make another place to hold
events like this—the snow, the lake,
and seeing it, reflecting if you like
upon this show is still this show.)

(A snow globe held at home
upon the mantelpiece—ironic purchase
to ironically memorialize a trip
where tourist feels apart from self
and from the destination both—so
shake the globe as if to register intentionality
contained in an exemplary universe in miniature
with still unique white plastic chips
that swirl and eddy over the now golden
Tour d'Eiffel, monument to industry
Outliving its initial task to mark the centre
Of a temporary festival—snow and the

Empty streets—not even made to resemble
But to replace ironically a memory
Made in another country by a company
Employing workers' memories bent toward assembly).

The Knight Adventurer

We must think of a weightless mobility
Peculiar to the knight errant
A bodiless doll in crinoline
Held up by a bodiless doll

And upon us a horse with a whisper
That opens the gate of our stall
A warmth from the mumbling lips
That breathes on the neck of the doll

Mince and roar, mince and roar
Across the dark tableau
A bat in a glass-fronted cabinet
pinned over the watermeadow

Christ in his moment of glory
Flies over the houses and wells
In a tunic resembling Christmas
Festooned with baubles and bells

The dolls and the bat and the Jesus
Put away in a drawer for the night
As the parrots and monkeys and persons
Collect what they can of themselves

Horrendous adventures await us
As stories we tell to the wall
A lover is shaving her arm pits
In a globe of gold light down the hall

Sitting around the round table
And speaking the names of themselves
The venturous heroes of selfhood
Trade tokens of meaningful tales

At last comes the time of the blackbird
Stood highest of all on his bough
And lifting his heart to the tip of his beak
He begins once again to recall

With no words to suggest it has meaning
The knights are perplexed by his song
But the longer he sings his anthem
The less they remember themselves

The moon has been present all evening
A face at once poignant and dull
As the last of the gold and the last of the blue
Disappear in the notes of his tune

He sings to the end of our history
In absolute bliss and disdain
A day when the world has stopped meaning
And returned to itself in a dream.

Salvator Mundi

The arm that held the light slowly
Lowered it behind the desk edge
Of the ocean—turning the brilliant sheet surface
From gold to depthless blue

The curtain was held back
Or let to fall as mournful sound
Of curlews filled into
The raised canopy

The room came furnished thus
A lived-in look that I returned
As sun rose on a burnished plate
Upon the breakfast set

The tea palace is little more
Than fantasy—a bag of leaves
Stored for a future tea party
I can't attend (wind and spoon stirred)

The arm falters the light
The sheet ripples the dark
Snags across its horizon
The stars the moon

Pareidolia

A moon erected thus—her doppelgänger smile
Silver island wincing in the well
Indistinguishable from
A discarded shell. A face

The trees smell like flesh
In bloom—as dogs shit underneath
We are in unison with
Our own decaying wish

Coleridge's Window

The frost performs its secret ministry
unhinged by any part. I can't
recall a single day as any thing
beyond a spectacle of loss. One
has the instant almost held of course
and one has the bliss of ignorant
forgetfulness—but who is that
and what of any of it now—it is
come to facts and facts do not exist
in company to selves—they are a
sheen of details on the lens of one
blank window bordering the inside with the out.

having early left one never can
relive the prior instant or relieve
the action of its consequence.
Man, being timely, sticks in time
no counterfactual chances—ghosts
that never walked the house
                        haunt everyday.

Cycling in a cypress grove

aroused and all appalled
in sudden agony the soul
(the mind prophetic of some future state)
I feel the mark upon
my absent trouser leg—

The shin placed by the cog
the foot falling just so
grand as life, small as the next act
cognition—recognition—soiled cloth.
I begin thus with myself.

poète maudit

a pair of green trousers
cannot save you from despair
even the right colour
sat in the right chair

I shall fall over
comical and fat
rolling between tables
an embarrassment

the small flat I rent
filled with pretence
objets and éditions
bought at great expense

a whiff of posh cologne
a jingle of Schubert
nothings gilt with shit
alone.

Bible stories before bed

Throughout the seas and hillside floods
all creatures breast the torrents
after their own kind. Whichever way
in folly aimed at Death,
that witless tyrant—all are bent on life.
And life it is that teems their multitudes
across the exsiccated plains.

The sound of the imaginary flute
I can't hear anything
as sounds peal through their resonance
high notes above the dancing bear
that I can't possibly see
in my current circumstance
his girdle tooled red leather and his muzzle
weaved of basketry—a small tired black bear from the Urals
dancing on all fours until encouraged
to stand proud: a mock human the humans mock
to mock themselves. The flute, the flute
the bear the flute the bear.

*

A white bear and a ragged staff
the stage is empty and the audience
see fog and fire—an air raid 30 miles off—
Coventry Cathedral, Warwickshire

*

So many dead and so few
that I knew properly—a handful only
being mother, 3 uncles & 2 aunts
but of their passing very little—and enough

Puberty

The self-loathed sister naked in the hall
I hear the creaking like a human moan
Her breasts are hidden by a paper towel
Her mound the moon of Venus shines

Wet hair
Hers is an anguish she self-clasped
An agony held tight—on pause—the bath
Is owl white—a dreadful clamour rinses her despair.

The Selve Obscured

Following a straight line
He finds himself
Lost somewhere in words obscured

The error was in noticing
Hand-written warnings
Drawn on every tree

Here there are no more lions
No more leopards & no snakes
Imaginary leaves fall from the air

Leaves that obscure
The path he leaves
The undergrowth is overgrown

The forest made of woods
Where convalescent glades
Pushed through with avenues

The city grows to look like trees
The people like the child
Abandoned in the woods

Tell me a story of the tree-lined path
Generations hear the tale
That's all.

*

I started noticing
Small things
The yellow submarine
& insect world

A multi-coloured
Match stick flare
An indigo toy legionnaire
Accompanied my fantasy

Hero of the desert
To command
A post-war England
Emptying of rural charm

*

By faith endure
because my animal is close
I grow incorporate
with loss

The wandering grave
we perch upon
as if we have
a destination

*

A car reverses
over us
the dark garage
the underpass

Perish the thought
perish the wings
a small ship
founders in the waves

But then another
and another sail
I do not see
come into view

*

My Dad's Cortina
parked outside
the freshly tarmacked drive
in 1972

The West Brom scarf (contrasting night and day)
this spitfire doll
all wrapped in tinsel
for the winter festival

The barge proceeds
upon the midnight Ouse
to gangplanks that
alight in bluey black

50 years on
most families long gone
or parents lived and died
in the same home

My mind
a whisper past
the quiet road
behind the pines

The end of poetry

The owl of Hegel
Eyeing knowledge sees
A posthumous existence
In a twilight wood

Whatever that owl means
It does not matter in the end
Death closes down the gap
Between.

The ghost of Egremont appears in a snapshot of his favourite horse

Egremont is vanished—
Flaxen mane on fire—
A sodden moor in sepia
The horse rears at a flare

That did not appear
Until the photograph
exposed a subtle form
standing next to her

Various late landscapes

Eoan clouds of pinky
green, greeny pink
a colour I can see
's impossible
one above the other
touching not quite
night above the drinking pond
below as bats pass close
to their invisible
reflections twittering
a nighttime version of
a cricket song.
When will the sadness visit
long enough for
these vast pettinesses to wash off?

Love was meant to be robust
and irresistible
not timid as a dragonfly
I cannot see. Night sighing
like a satisfaction it cannot have known
the virtue of a sentiment must be
its appropriate proximity to what takes place
the brisk reflection skittering
Love was meant to be
as real as passing by
a pond at night I cannot see.

From the west
a question passes as
the pink turns grey
the trees are filling up
their deep blue Prussian ink
I can't begin

again to single out the shade
for my forgotten purpose
seeing that the midges have
now disappeared along with
Trakl and Corot.

Colder still
tomorrow's breaking light
lit from another sun
takes a crack
at settling the dreary
sob. Half afternoon
a stranger falling down
outside the shop. I care
enough to carry on

Cows move like a barrow mound
over the hedge
wet saggy weight
stood in the field
a drinking trough
with darkness curdled round.

Next comes the twitch
announcing summer in the insect world
How can an ant
How can an elephant recall
the exact ground
east west west east
to there establish
all this passing shit

Christobel goes wading in the dark
laughing at her own impracticality
I've worn a frown in mother's dress
we kneel and watch the froth accumulate
or is she crying I can't tell

neither can she
it's irresistible to drown
after a supper on the beach
why else eat squid
unless you want to be a sea creature
I'd rather drown than be a fig
a toothbrush and some cake left in the room
being parched we walk
across two miles of sand towards the sea
the sun is rising making this the East
scalloped dunes where god forgot to hide
our blisters are stigmata
just as any wound is earned upon the earth
we bend down to the waves we can't control
our needs a pornographic flare
entering the atmosphere
illuminating its own death.
*Saudade, Soledad, rimpiangere,
gabbiano in lacrime…gabbiano che ride.*

*

The East wind of Ignacio blowing hot
The fish like slurry pouring from the net
The West upends the cavalry, fat colonels in their finery
The circus ends.

*

I act to catch the falling glass
I don't
the moon is still extant
along the coast the wind
wraps through the trees
all writhing in an ecstasy
daylight is bitter bright

the mothy mouth, the creaking bed
I am surrounded by the dogs
Who cannot tell what month it is
But know they do not know the child
Who passes by the door just now
I will survive. I won't, the world
it won't and much as I do anything
I don't.

*

There is a snake
under the deck
it lives there
until dark

I starved myself
a week
so I could talk
to it

Under the boards
under the stars
I hear it listening
but cannot speak.

*

Cameras record our souls
as Veronese drew a saint
the paint somehow electrical
as if the body had a role.

(Sea Poems)

A faint sea on the wind withdraws
the air a broad salt blade
tastes bloody as the warm sun drops
and races up the beach to wear my face

shade soon to be followed
sleepily by dark—we've
been all day relieved of work
or any meaningful task
now only food—the flush
of too much sun and wind and rain
settles on our mood
slumbering the mind as if
it were the last day of the year
in someone's life.

High beyond the panicked sea
gull scream
a grey smear thumbs
the yellow heights and here
beneath
a singular last voice
calls out to reach its other self

What would you cry out
if you held
the silence of the world
in your cracked throat

a broken sparrow ruffled on the road
a plastic bag gambolling up the street

Hither waking on the glaucous plain,
beach before dawn after rain
a pale puke-coloured dessert
with micro-beads and dabberlocks

Retch a dragoon of vodka sea
salt and the history of an individual
etched upon my withered tongue.
Spring starts the tale of self-improvement!

A song writ off Aphasia's coast
where unnamed bloated wrecks
wash up in angelic suds. We're
only here for a short time

putting together proper nouns:
wahoo, petrel, viviparous eelpout,
we thread a worthy epitaph nobody reads
because the seismograph's red ink ran out

Proteus old man
an ocean in a pail
who cannot help himself
but fall, as all the risen waves will fall.

Summoned and subsumed
A nacreous aphrodisiac
His spittle on the sand
Where scattered seashells skittle to and fro.

Shipwrecked satyrs baulking at the tide
Vomit morning's reckoning: green bile
Matted mane on futtock shrouds
Gaskin strained. Unheard alarum bells.

dunnock soaked in coastal squall

October allotment where

redstarts left in September

blackberries in season still

sea up on the stones
or is it cars that pass
we're always hearing something
we can only guess

the midwife enters with her weights
to make a record of the birth
in time to unwind the umbilical link
between the blue-faced baby and

the mother's warm Mediterranean sack
—drawn into the world
a red-brown whale
drowns on the land.

who is besides me now
her gradual vanishing
leaves a vacancy
the same size as the sea.

we find ourselves
foolish on this side
writhing in
what might be

if she hadn't died if we had
a helicopter ride over the trees
drowning out the words
I didn't say.

The Blind Whale

Out in the smoky harbour
mines bob up and down
and words and scraps of words and ghosts
go walking into town

out on the frosty moor
heather twinkles code
and black grouse lek to find a mate
and red grouse scratch the ground

out in the morning ocean
twenty miles from land
the sea-pig swims along alone
dreaming of herring and squid

on the outskirts of town
a fox goes through the bins
emptying out Saturday night
pizza and bottles and cans

on the pebbly seafront
washed up in the storm
a metal steamer trunk
covered in seaweed and foam

we wander along the shale
and happen upon the box
what we hoped to find, and failed to find
neither of us can recall

The Blind Whale

The world outside itself
an accident occurred
and we became occasion of
an unprecedented word

A glistening whale eye rises
pulled in with both arms
drop it bloody on the boat
wet like a new born child

Or say a syllable arrives
And you can't help its sound
Nor comprehend a purpose
To bend your mind around

The rescue boat arrives
And circumscribes the corpse
Floating in the bay
What more is there to say?

Letters from the Interior

And saw the Earth as finitesimal.

The carcass of an eagle rotting in the vale.

Ancient oak tree crumbles into paste eventually.

The sun will fade, the planet break.

Fried egg on the patio.

A moth might fly over the mountain peak.

And nothing that the thoughtful gentleman achieves will alter anything.

Sending this nostalgic letter home, though having left there without wishing to return.

How can another day be happening.

Sat around a fire consuming more than just the wood it feeds upon.

A riverbed more like an argument for chaos than intention.

I had thought I hated my school uniform, but what else should I wear?

Certainly the petty fashions that consumed me are now gone, but with them, perhaps so am I?

I still always wear a jacket. What would be the alternative? Someone else's jacket?

Why an education would seem a fit preparation for anything other than itself becomes less and less apparent.

I had held onto a fountain pen of my father's for years, and then, giving it away to someone who was unburdened by its sentimental value, I felt almost elation; light-headed and aware that my own life was worth just as little.

It was too great a responsibility. So give it away.

Accumulating memories to what end (other than the obvious one)?

A squab pierced by a spear cooked outdoors is as delicious as any newfangled offering.

I was still expecting the small tributaries of wrinkles ringed around my wrists to disappear so that my hands might recover their familiar youthful appearance.

A soft acknowledgment of a stranger's beauty rather than a physical shock: at last, desire has petered out, overwhelmed by experience.

Accumulated wealth like storing old leaves.

Those handful of favourites, four or five poets that still matter, and yet, this room filled with thousands of books. It's like living on a piss-rank midden, hide-bound corpses waiting, like automata, to be whispered into a pretend existence.

And with the few last remaining poets you must be careful. If you find that you read one and the language is now inert, then the number is one fewer. Dwindle dwindle on your pile.

All the while, a walk through unobserved phenomena, does it matter that I do not recognize the trees? It seems that my walks in the country now are really walks through a catalogue of missing names.

And what of painters pushing paint around, egg and oil, a slowly rotting salad for the soul.

Bronzino's green silk backdrop; the fallen lances of the rout of San Romano; saddest dog contemplates dead nymph; purple buzz of mountain meets the deadpan sky; doomed figure faces lake; water from the old tap twists and angles into Belfast sink; blue-eyed Doge; bull beneath sheer cliff; elm illuminated in bright sunlight; old lady with her tea pot set; leaping hares and hunters in the nighttime woods; sunflowers like the heads of martyred saints; her cat laps milk, her legs apart; the Putney house, the sere canal, the withered Stuka, rows of burned out crops.

It all goes to hell.

And still, in some of these old pools, pike older than the surrounding buildings that they will never see. Two hundred year old houses come and go. Dynasties decay thank god.

The lurid nylon baling twine
in greens and reds and clemantine
circumambulates the globe
intentional or otherwise.

England obsessed with these dour memorials and anniversaries: a brief moment of national pride and pseudo-security nestled between the lunatic catastrophes of war. What of the absurdity of these famous historical disasters, where are those anniversaries, those monuments?

My two years child with a flint of fear held fast in his tiny fist. Where did that come from?

Morning walk in the unknown city. Excitement in search of consumption. Dogged by the ubiquitous self. Enter a bar with anonymity's concomitant low status. Even here.

The uneventful party following the less than spectacular reception. Society is never where you are, even if you're there. All these toadies are contemptible, and even worse still, the cynical attendee.

If I had to relate one main purpose for my extended exile I couldn't. Much has happened. That's the meat of it. I have the unsettling impression that I have been misled, mostly by myself, for whom I can offer little in the way of genuine fondness. I have no sense that any alternative course of action would have led anywhere more satisfactory. In short, it is here, where I am not at home, and it might as well be, because nowhere would suffice. Exile is a grand way of saying fuck all.

A strong sense this morning that I ought not to leave the house, mitigated by the concern that if I chose to indulge such a notion today, I might well never leave. Either way.

Birds hiding under a very mediocre carpark shrub. Only sentimentality can offer them a status higher than a mite.

Same for humans.

Caravaggio and Tassi. Your call on their contributions to the argument. Church decoration and other crimes. Beauty in corruption. A moral chiaroscuro. We do feebly if we ask a painter for moral guidance.

What I can't quite yet grasp is that this is what will have been my life. And that even under pressure, aware of the obvious time constraints, the fact remains that I often fail to choose what I most likely would prefer, even if simply available.

Gentileschi and Anguissola.

The thought-experiments that led to the theory of clinamina. Suggestive of free will or of an unpredictable randomness that might be thought of as such.

The consolations of orthodoxy: the consolations of heterodoxy.

Without the prize of free will can there be any moral responsibility? Do we hedge our bets?

The sparrow nor the mite give care.

Art folds the dust into endless patterns.

Golden eyeless fish adorn the polygonal mudcracks.

I open the car door and step out into the slushy road. If it was intended, it was nonetheless unwilled. And the pavement? And the spill of neon from the dark interior?

Moments of Inertia

Regarding the interior

The light of Solomon and the blind Samson
reels between the pillars—a martyr to pride
and the jawbone of an ass. I wish to begin
again—to unfling the crumbs of a moments past feast.

Love has disguised itself—come creeping in the camp at night
A merchant in a veil with nothing but the need to sell
Am I alone in wanting her to leave and never to have come
A small boy woken by the din stands in the shadow and is gone.

We reach out to the radiation as an after glow
And carrots grow three limbs instead of one. I
Can't react to the increasing damage I have done
But somehow muster sympathy for my own skeleton.

Samson Beleaguered (His blindness/Death)

A terrible haircut
For the interview
His father's shirt
The suit brand new

The train delayed
Because of traffic
Arriving late
In a blind panic

*

If he tried to recall
A specific scene
As the impulse
Of writing truthfully
What would that matter
In this world?

The bars of the heater
Throw an orange glow
Onto his face in the frigid gloom
With the bedroom window
Coated in ice, he can barely make out
The falling snow

A blue glass angel
an inch high bear
From the chemist shop
Appears in the air

Lifted by love
The cold-gloved mother

A yellow flower
Over the covers

As if his eyes
were beads of water
And the day
a breeze blown over

Always recall
Her kindness towards
Him above all
Often forget

Taking his hand
In an avenue of limes
with a glass of cool water
left by the heater

Blossom and snow
wheels through the air
Enough of the building
remains to appear

A once grand house
abandoned for years
Do not enter
tacked to the door

A diet of feathers and
a diet of flies
as his bare hands hang
through the chain link wires

Coleridge's Mirror

this small desert island
winter in England
a disaster with soot
as old as the house is

cut in half
the mirror wall
exhausting the terror
of falling over.

Hall lamp suspended
Six feet above
A moth on the rug
Young enough

To fit under the table
& lick the leg

Reading on the afternoon bed
Let my feet get freezing cold

A square of yellow—a triangle of green
Then mauve then death our truest friend

Wreck of the Sisterland

Boats boast across the skein
Skinny mast a cross masters
The wind sheets of rain
Skin the winding sheet remains

When in lust we drown
Downed a lashing—weather
The leather hide—wet inside
Her lengthening—lists to one side

She males replace the dream
She'd made—a moon's face
Then the sun's reflection
Deemed too close to the room's embrace

I can't recall in darkness
The damp rat barks in the hall
Red-eyed cunts—the dank carpet
Car headlights—rolled up wet joint.

Sister on her haunches over the pit
style shitter after bad peaches
Her hairy cream paunch and bear tattoo
Strain as she drains her spew & shit

Permanent loss—the beach recedes
Past the post of private property
Sperm enters the host—reaches
The ocean held for public use

Her pubis—the untying of a gown
After sickness and the tidying self groom
With warm flannel—rich green cotton
Turns brown—ready to reach again.

Stiff-pricked afternoon—a study
Shuttered from the day—barely a view
Sliver of thigh white against van dyke brown
Palming the rose tip stuttered into use.

*

Then teapot tea—fuck you me ol' China—go for Darjeeling—
from the larder—read the leaves—feeling lucky
that I'm on a journey—marriage, marriage failure, Death—then later
After tea the quick descent—tears or yawns, then laughter.

The Turk's head

Winter drinking throngs the pub
Beer supports the spinning room's hubbub
Eleven thirty trickles out our sobs
Final round turfed out into the swoon.

Thrill wheels when she reaches after me
swelling hope desires wherever next
I'm so grateful to become so lost
In such temporary settings—loins, lions, fires, Romantic ghosts.

The Dardanelles

So Crispin never struck out with his arms
against the torrent and the swell
Nor did he seek the nature of his soul
But saw his eighty-ninth solstice in
Protected by his own invisibility
The surface of the sea unbroken
A token celebration in his private rooms.

Unheimlich

There lies a meadow heimlich in the wood
A house we know where we have never been
I see a girl crossing the meadow path
And hand in hand with her I see myself

*

the wolf exhumes the grandmother
reluctantly but lacking choice
transgressions necessary for the plot
to shift to the next chapter the next scene

*

the lover leaves the room,
the house, the capital,
to visit nana in her pram
baking with her apron on

Bathetic verse

The blind girl is wearing
A white and yellow dress
Her eyelashes look delicate
In her sunken eye sockets
I watch her fold her cane
And drop it out of reach
She might be 20 but
her mother wipes her mouth
(she bit her lip while eating flan)

the woman I met
at the memorial
was still so sad
about *her* father's death
her slightly twisted teeth
her hair pulled back
I might have fallen for

Narcissus's scissors

Iris eyes itself in deep green robes
Situated at the centre of the bank
And raising up a vase with which to hold
Its flower suicided blue and gold

The Last Supper

The heart is crazy in its cage
and yet each evening we begin
with the same speech
and one half glass of chocolate milk
with one bruised peach
the inability of language
to describe the unknown other
it inevitably fails to reach

The object observed (D**th)

       Having fallen into
       The sea I obviously
Obviously can't be saved
       For How Long?
       Wave upon wave
Wave. The anguish of love
         Like the poor foolish seal looking up
         Looking up to see what almost
What it almost knows it cannot
         Having stepped into the crevasse
         The chasm of deep blue green
Having fallen asleep at the wheel
         The collar I feel at my neck
         Is the cold hand of despair.
Despair the hands at my throat
         The saltwater scarf that I wear
         That I only know this upon
The occasion of my death. The
         Occasion upon which I die.

The evening otherwise

I step right into
Your cherry-scented chaos

Jingle-jangle goes the chimes
Of Christmas-fuck-catastrophe

My darling wheelbarrow flaunts her grace
While newcomers besmirch her face

I'm not invited to the ball
And anyway I have a date

With Dr. Scotch and Fanny Wine
Up the stairs and down the hall.

The ghost of a poppy (Armistice Day, 2018)

The souls of plants go walking
        seeds ground like a god
nothing to be seen
        but sod covered remains

Immortal stalk—dried parent
        sitting in his chair
reading history to himself
        to justify the present

dying to be quiet
        no longer in the room
myth died when Apollo 11
        landed on the moon

a gurgling barbarous kraut or jew?
who came from accidental here
his ear against the graveyard wall
whether dane or dutch returning home
to plant his bones beneath an ancient yew

what shall be tamed, what gets hurled?
his is now a world that has no tune
and empty fame replaces empty self
were duty calling surely he'd have heard
he'll return to heaven to undo his birth.

Song endings

Everybody says the war is over
sipping gin along the slappy river

Waking to a wasted life
gripped by the hilarious fear of self

Dog looks at me I look at him
neither particularly certain what it means

After a while even pain is dull
the coffee carafe half-full

*

Letter to a comrade

on the nature of Art and the grand consolations of Love

The expression was one
of mordant fatigue
a being disposed
to accuracy

I can't be described
as anything but
The outcome of
a functional fuck

Motherest dear
and fathering Tom
fashioning a
productive fusion

atoms swerve
to be seen
a clinamen is
observed as I'm

obscene as I am
a pompous baboon
I'm irritated when
irritating
friends out of ten
marks out of sync
the laughter comes in through the walls.

If its love you're after
then what was before
a shrew in a tea cup
a pin in a shoe
the house is on fire
a comforting scene
the police can't gain entrance
to ransack the tale
we victims have nothing to tell.

Dead hand on my arm
writing dead sonnets
for dead volunteers
I'm grateful the marbles
have poured down the stairs
I'm grated against
The little hall table
My face is an ecstatic mask.

Love as a filter
protecting the game
of a bucket of selfhood
sloshing the rug
don't be down-hearted

if it turns out to fail
there's always the jug to re-fill.

*

Watch the dancing foreigner
try to read my article

The flight's delayed
my pant leg frayed
the meat unrecognizable

*

(Writing this and leaving out
all I meant to say instead)

Even an outcome can't kill chaos
the baked Alaska melts before the Aga

Between the Angels (non-existent) & the beast
between pure knowledge (non-existent) & desire

*

their ears that are pink with the light
as the morning enters their room
in his dream they are lying apart
the head coming out of the briefs
to his mouth in the hotel suite
wet with a glistening strand
to finish him off with a gulp
and wipe on the back of the hand

*

the jewish girl must be
somebody else's belle
my hand inside her gown
as if invited to

*

I caught a firefly in a jar
And held it there for my delight
It glowed inside for half an hour
And then was dark as night

*

An angel plays the oboe
Another the bassoon
I cannot hear their orchestra
Their symphony or tune

I see them on the hilltop
As clear as it were day
I know no reason for their show
But pleasure in their play

*

Forest lights the escapees thru
a panicked thought of freedom
hidden moments of the night
are written in their movements

*

A house upon the stairs
we pass it in a haze
mounted in the grey-
green coloured emptiness

*

a cheap tattoo of Halifax
drawn across my face
no what nor why available
to clarify my choice

*

The lichen on the Easter Island heads
The mould upon the medieval tome
The blue cheese eaten after lunch
My feet look ghostly white beneath the foam

*

On the street gurney
Wheeled into oncoming traffic I
Feel no fear the lights are beautiful
And those that pushed me seemed so sensible

*

my mother died at the flower stall
died in the wool of the handmade stole
died at the stand of vegetables
a wreath of cabbage in her hair

*

Lives of the Painters

born on St. Marks St.
EC1. Whitechapel
What is left
of the painter's egg.
the broken pencil

sketch a jug
the end of rituals
wander dead
close to the Wittenham Clumps

*

the crow creaks on repeat
a Devonshire farmer long like me
has sent me a jacket of wool and tweed
gold & red and green it is.
It turns out not to fit.

*

The last thing I recall
Is hearing others chatter
In a language I can almost
piece together

*

Lives of the Painters

Willow in a tree
A human figure
Moves ahead of
What I see, until
A line draws
Her back to light
Life-like

*

Coming into Manhattan
The mysterious smile on the face of the sun

And the bridge under the river severs
As I watch the local strangers run

*

i.m. Mark Hollis (Talk Talk)

from South End Green in North West L
to his girlfriend's flat in Muswell Hill
listening to Bob Marley and Carl Orff
wrote a song and shared a spliff

*

we had come to the cake
for a couple of years
we ate lemon and rind
and the shells that we found

*

the frog prince sits in Brooklyn Heights
his vest a dingy grey
he listens mostly to Schubert
on library LPs

*

I might have a sherry
While the rain outside
Fills the void
I'll fill my glass again

*

the slowest slug
and millipede

at night make progress
through the weeds

unnaturally floodlit
the forest where
the bear and antelope
are scarce

a boat I dunno about
left in a field
rotted through'n
mice eaten

ostracods huddle
in a Bedfordshire puddle
450m yrs older
than man

when we leave
through dewy grass
a green wake walked
through silver waves

a heavy rose bows
against its weight
a blossom face
blows and bends and aches

I've waited here
Quietly
Anxious
And empty

*

The Emptiness Song

Almighty nothing
planted upside down
out in the shocked wilderness
a bear tears thru my hrt

More average kids
into the world
indifferent to life
indifferent to art

More hrs of loneliness
placed nowhere
forgetting nothing
matters here

yr love
did not feel optional

felt huge and tiny
every day

My sadness is
the finished meal
and gathered strangers
in the hall

*

When it was night
I had nowhere
to go like opening
to let the outside in

If I fell against living
then only death

It was brave of her
to go first

Opened herself
to set me down
exhausted
in my first and final bed

I can't forget her
emptiness
it was true
before my memory

Yesterday feels
just the same
an animal
I can't really know

All I can do
is try not to be
too waylaid
by what I am

Most people seem
to close me off
so I try not
to let them

Everywhere I go
I come back to
remembering that
I was once you

That's why I love
the sea so much
it's everything
we ever were

*

a pigeon flew into my eye
where it lived for a year and a half
the stories it told me were false
but at least it was a good laugh.

*

the search costs of finding a mate
I lift my head over the gate
The first face I see is familiar to me
But it seems that I got here too late.

*

a feather garden where
where finches come to die
the tiny corpses I
I never see them there

a single thread
4 thousand meters long
of silk in one
cocoon

the pre-existent form
of this old oak
is somewhere
hidden in a disappeared acorn

the sky bright aluminium
after a rain shower
forgotten self
for this last hour

a headless bust
seen through the hedge
his shoulders smooth as marble
his throat vulnerable

boschi sacri
tige de lavande
búho bramido
ende der Menge

the sphinx is blind in the snow
she flies around the house
dead upon the ground
another endless song

Moments of inertia

I've always been flattered by a bourgeois air
even while tuning my bass guitar

to English punk
the trick is to succeed

and not be seen courting it
(even as you mock success as shit)

I just want to be adored by someone hot
pretending I'm not shallow, even if I'm not.

Does the dog love me? I'd be fine
if she died. She's not even mine.

(Val Raworth mocked the Beatles for
being middle class to a roomful of

middle class Marxist poets from
Cambridge. Are

The Kinks any more authentic
because their school was less expensive?

I went to a shitty comprehensive
though I ended up at university

Reading Donne and Keats *is* the establishment
even as I flash a little class resentment)

If I'm jealous of more successful poets
I make some effort not to show it

And even if I read their verse
I'm certain that it's probably worse

But as I don't believe in great artists or
anyone being better than anyone else anymore

The purpose of all this seems to be
the wrong way to think about reality.

Get on with it, get out the way.
The woman I love ignores me most the day

It's fine mostly. I thought I wanted more *amour*
but breakfast comes and goes without

A fight, we fix our bowls, we sit, we eat
we hardly ever shout. Or speak.

My advice, which I don't take
be true to yourself, even if you think you're fake.

*

I'm tired of this palaver, spitting gobs of phlegm
pulling on a pullover and heading out of town

Hard to be a self when self's soon overwhelmed
exhausting the authentic before its even noon

If I loved you madly would you be my muse
then I'd drop you in the lake and head back for a nap

Bye bye musey, you nasty vacant ruse
I hate us both for being us, and talking all this crap.

Thus more self-pitying soliloquies
hunt out an audience we fail to please.

A bowl of sloppy goop is all
we manage to resemble as we fall.

*

The fact that I don't like any of you is mitigated
by the fact that I don't know most of you so you don't know you're hated.

It is also true that I don't much like myself
though I've maintained a habit of supporting him

And siding with his aimless acts
and often dubious, misleading, self-defeating/self-promoting claims.

*

Congratulate yourself for being kind
in a situation where you offer little

To a passing stranger
or a family friend

And the enduring sense that they are rude
and that the world lacks gratitude

reminds you that you must forget yourself
and never hope.

*

What were you hoping to get out of this
you'll be dead in thirty years or less

All those fellow players that you charmed
have disappeared into the arms of other idiots

So there will not be
a reunion with lovers you don't see

Or payback for the douches who
outnumber any other group you know.

*

This shiitake mushroom broth
tastes of socks and garden mulch

And yet it is delicious 'cos
I'm hungry and wasn't really expecting much for lunch.

*

She goes on another trip
I'll feed the dogs and empty out the shit.

It's sort of where I've ended up
a semi-temporary lodger with a semi-permanent half-decent job

*

Why does the gloomy turtle sing
how can it bury its disdain

While on the rug the lovers grapple and refrain
from any mention of their obvious inanity

I can no longer hover here
above the lapping waves that hinder my evaporation

Into hopeless moments strung between
tight pockets filled with obsolete denominations.

*

How can it fly without sufficient wings
or without wishing to be seen

Its alter-ego burrows underground
which gives a sense of where it ought to have been.

*

Perhaps the world is coming to an end
perhaps it already has and no one said

We were wandering the beach at low tide
Looking for any evidence it might provide

Hoping Hero might one day return,
To share with us the value of his journey

but he had already arrived and gone
back to his house which had become a restaurant

His family's dead he now forgets just why
he left, but recognizes a recipe

It is a simple soup, in which his tears drop
he tears some bread to soak up the last dregs of broth.

*

Forgetting being and forgetting all the world
for most of the days and yet retaining self.

Not unhappy with the signalled dawn
nor joyous as the sun sets at sunset.

La notte è nera e blu
the colours blur.

Il tramonto è rosa e oro
un verde che non ho mai visto.

*

Each move was seen
as reaching in
to the abysmal pond

and shaking mountains
with the hand
without intent yet formed.

The idle ripples on the surface
brought us to our own reflection

The statue searches for her son
the crowd applauds their kiss

What is it grants us peace
a story then some lunch

My mother wanders to her grave
we pack her snack (as she'd packed ours)

And wave her on her way
assured that she is nowhere now

and we will join her there someday.

The Bird Zone

And my father's face, on his death-bolster, had seemed to hint at some form of aesthetics relevant to man

—Samuel Beckett

Anonymous motorway café

Anonymous motorway café
generic cup & saucer on metallic tray
cheaply produced alloy knife & spoon
I notice that the moon has permanently gone

Knight of clubs advance
Into the unknown fight
You cannot fight a dance
Against a hidden clown

*

Death of memory

Lived through the war
Now his is gone
Memory a curse and remedy
Is loss and where we hold her from
Half of my mind is fulminating
Half is locked away
The turtle dove that sits
Was sitting yesterday
Mournfully noting nothing
If I reach out now it is
To things like shingles
fallen from a roof

*

a boy walks down Hanbury lane
his mother's hand dropping him off
a boy walks past the line of elms
into a future dream

that generation has passed
and passing onto us
some ill-defined task
we fumble with and pass

all the people you have known
all those you loved have died
have died or watch as you now die
all of them have gone

your advice or more
just your enduring presence
when my world collapses
"you're tougher than this." Life is.

*

Bird in the rafters

Stanley, Idaho June 22nd 2020

There is a bird trapped in the loft
A flycatcher that flew in through the door
I've tried to catch him with a net

He's small and grey with yellow
On his belly and he's back & forth
Trying to find the right way out

I hear him quietly cry
Now he's on the stovepipe eyeing me
It looks as if he might escape at last

(as I write my father's dying
in a distant hospital)
Just now he's hopped onto the step

but stops and seems to look back in
& so I chased him out
I didn't want him trapped inside again.

*

Wanted to call again
One last time to say
What exactly? Nothing
That I haven't said.

Shrub Hill Station
For some reason
You and Ambrose
Sitting waiting for the London train

Meet you at Foubert's in Chiswick
(the yellow awnings long since gone)
Breakfast Sunday morning
Trying not to think

I put you through this
So many times
Leaving for another country
Making our goodbyes

He's too tired to talk
He sends his love
They'll ring
When he wakes up

*

My Father terrified by the sound of the curtain

Having survived
one close call

he struggles in bed
the curtain behind
his egg shell head
the rustling sound
reminding him of
something someone
he has not seen off.

*

It is the various lives
we did not follow
haunting us with
unknown loves and nearby sorrow

The rising (Lazarus)

Awkward as it is
Impossible
he has returned to us
as if from the past
held over his abyss
his frail arms flailed
and flew him back
to the near surface of the world
No food no drink
we were certain he was
on the brink until he turned
a slow pale shift
Not faith but instinct
as we were holding
offerings
bereft

The falling (Daedalus)

Hunched homunculus abandoned
on the bathroom floored
Daedalus' waxed wings melt
since hoisted by an uncontrollable desire
(what kind of musical accompaniment?
cicada lost to song or single magpie croak)
This desiccated ape
discarded by ambition
sought to emulate an ancient joy
an excavated jug whereon
an etched image of Medea
daughter of the sky and sea
who rejuvenates the old
such myths are long since buried
with the hope of soul or body gaining flight

(Misquoting the quotidian)

a magpie bounces on the lawn
bearing the colossal weight of life like light
you go to bed quite early now
I leave the blind open at night

The garden grows in universal drab
And smells of sweet & sickly mulch and lavender
The sky is empty like a hope
I cannot name—pale rose and alabaster white

Yesterday I thought that you had died
Today I make you lunch
I think I can't adjust to this
But bread and cheese still make a cheese sandwich

Only a garden could be called divine
But nature easily refuses such a silly name
The greatest prize we thought to give
Is nothing—nature isn't listening

(the one relief to me it seems
is none of this means anything)

(Twilight summer)

Sitting with my dying father
we know the stillness of the ether
after the birds' resounding vesper
above us out of sight we hear
a stranger in a tiny plane fly over
what we know, what's left to discover
we can't say, we just hover
in shared solitude for an hour
passing thoughts between each other
watching Phoebus-Apollo lower

The bird zone

A soft fluting sound that lifts last year's children back into the road.

Was nearly off and remembered that the ground was still perfect without me.

What I can't find is the first instance without which I would not belong.

Stay for just an hour and let me breathe.

If all our talk was transcribed into an instant would it resemble those trees?

Waiting for something that will make a difference, like existence or rain.

The house continues to move all through its life.

This morning on my walk I hear the bells of Sacred Heart coming from all directions, and down the ginnel meet a wren, a blackbird and a sparrow.

Deciduous worn elephantine path.

A death mask cast in wax.

Daedalus' feathers lifting off the roof.

Branch shadows dance over the blowing curtain.

And a blackbird I can hear somewhere hereabouts.

Sleep with a common frog under the bed and dream of magpies living in the attic.

Unimaginable until passing into memory.

There's death of course, but what is it you really fear?

Anonymous at birth anonymous at death.

A small part of you remains for a short while.

I could hear the rain on the roof, on the glass of the conservatory, and further the wind in the garden trees.

Then I could hear the wind racing over the town, out over the coombes, buffeting the sparse copses, churning up the dells.

I could hear the hills and then I could hear the mountains and breathe along the rivers to the salt sea squall and all this through the pulse and breath of a human body.

The slow ocean of the land where humanitas churns.

The laurel grove grows dark green through the walls.

In the tiny bedroom where I was born.

The laral grave.

Then time creeps slowly through, crumbling the memorials.

Even a desk to call my own.

I'm borrowing this pen & chair.

To see the temporary as my new home.

I would be happier if.

Never having left.

I could not find her house again.

He clears his throat as if to speak.

He has forgotten how to swallow, he's forgotten how to breathe.

It rains & then it shines, the pine trees dipping in and out.

A swoop of swallows drinking from the pool.

I flew back home without a prayer, without a shoe or with two pairs.

The plum tree's rotten with old fruit, last year's plums still on the branch.

This is like a time of war.

I'm writing stupid poems in my head.

An ash tree standing in the middle of the field.

A liquid robin's evening song.

Philomelos in the dark.

Our favourite bird's soliliquy.

The greenfinch looks as if it's lost.

Linnets lining almost every park.

You'd hear a chaffinch call before it flew.

From where I sit I see a crow and magpie argue on the neighbour's roof.

I turn to look at you.

And then the sky turns off.